IN HIS MUCH-ANTICIPATED FOLLOW-UP to *The Crown Ain't Worth Much*, poet, essayist, music critic, and *New York Times* bestselling author Hanif Abdurraqib has written a book of poems about how one rebuilds oneself after a heartbreak, the kind that renders them a different version of themselves than the one they knew. It's a book about a mother's death, and finally admitting that Michael Jordan pushed off in the '98 finals. It's about forgiveness, and how none of the author's black friends wanted to listen to "Don't Stop Believin.'" It's about wrestling with histories, personal and shared, and how black people can write about flowers at a time like this. Abdurraqib writes across different tones and registers, with humor and sadness, and uses touchstones from the world outside—from Marvin Gaye to Nikola Tesla to his neighbor's dogs—to create a mirror, inside of which every angle presents a new possibility.

CUTTER: *I knew a sailor once, got tangled in the rigging. We pulled him out, but it took him five minutes to cough. He said it was like going home.*

THE PRESTIGE

the poem begins not where the knife enters

but where the blade twists.

Some wounds cannot be hushed

no matter the way one writes of blood

& what reflection arrives in its pooling.

The poem begins with pain as a mirror

inside of which I adjust a tie the way my father taught me

before my first funeral & so the poem begins

with old grief again at my neck. On the radio,

a singer born in a place where children watch the sky

for bombs is trying to sell me on love

as something akin to war.

I have no lie to offer as treacherous as this one.

I was most like the bullet when I viewed the body as a door.

I'm past that now. No one will bury their kin

when desire becomes a fugitive

between us. There will be no folded flag

at the doorstep. A person only gets to be called a widow once,

and then they are simply lonely. The bluest period.

Gratitude, not for love itself, but for the way it can end

without a house on fire.

This is how I plan to leave next.

Unceremonious as birth in a country overrun
by the ungrateful living. The poem begins with a chain
of well-meaning liars walking one by one
off the earth's edge. That's who died
and made me king. Who died and made you.

If your hate could be turned into electricity, it would light up the whole world.

—NIKOLA TESLA

Never mistake what it is for what it looks like.

—TERRANCE HAYES

To The City I Left // To The City I Left // To The City That Took Me Back

Published by Tin House, Portland, Oregon

Distributed by W. W. Norton & Company

Library of Congress Cataloging-in-Publication Data

Names: Willis-Abdurraqib, Hanif, author.
Title: A fortune for your disaster / Hanif Abdurraqib.
Description: First U.S. edition. | Portland, Oregon : Tin House, 2019.
Identifiers: LCCN 2019013318 | ISBN 9781947793439 (pbk.)
Classification: LCC PS3623.I57748 A6 2019 | DDC 811/.6—dc23
LC record available at https://lccn.loc.gov/2019013318

First US Edition 2019
Printed in the USA
Interior design by Jakob Vala

www.tinhouse.com

A FORTUNE FOR YOUR DISASTER

POEMS BY HANIF ABDURRAQIB

TIN HOUSE / Portland, Oregon

CONTENTS

THE TURN

THE PRESTIGE

THE PLEDGE

I want you so badly / but you could be anyone

—FLORENCE WELCH

IT IS ONCE AGAIN THE SUMMER OF MY DISCONTENT & THIS IS HOW WE DO IT

is creeping out of some open window same way it was in the summer of '95 when my heartbreak was a different animal howling at the same clouds & the cops broke up the block party at franklin park right before the song hit the last verse because someone from the right hood locked eyes with someone from the wrong one & me & my boys ran into the corner store & tucked the chocolate bars into the humid caverns of our pants pockets & later licked the melted chocolate from its sterling wrappers in the woods behind mario's crib with the girls we liked too much to want to know if they liked us back & there it was, the summer i learned to kiss the air & imagine it bending into a mouth & here it is again, the summer everything i love outside is melting & i tell my boys there is a reason songs from the '90s are having a revival & it's because the heart & tongue are the muscles with the most irresistible histories & i'm kind of buzzed. i'm kind of buzzing. i'm kind of a hive with no begging & hollow cavities. there is intimacy in the moment where the eyes of two enemies meet. there is a tenderness in knowing what desire ties you to a person, even if you have spent your dreaming hours cutting them a casket from the tree in their mother's front yard. it is a blessing to know someone wants a funeral for you. a coming together of your people from their faraway corners to tell some story about your thefts & triumphs. all of your better selves shaking their heads over a table, chocolate staining their teeth. i suppose there is also intimacy in the moment when a lover becomes an enemy, though it is tougher to say when it happens. probably when there is a song you can't remember them living inside of anymore, even if both of you curled your lips around the words in a car at some impossible hour of morning, driving away from the place you met. i like my agony threaded together by the same chorus. not everything is Sisyphean. no one ever wants to imagine themselves as the boulder.

HOW CAN BLACK PEOPLE WRITE ABOUT FLOWERS AT A TIME LIKE THIS

dear reader, with our heels digging into the good
mud at a swamp's edge, you might tell me something

about the dandelion head & how it is not a flower itself
but a plant made up of many small flowers at its crown

& lord knows I have been called by what I look like
more than I have been called by what I actually am &

I wish to return the favor for the purpose of this
exercise. which, too, is an attempt at fashioning

something pretty out of seeds refusing to make anything
worthwhile of their burial. size me up & skip whatever semantics arrive

to the tongue first. say: that boy he look like a hollowed-out grandfather
clock. he look like a million-dollar god with a two-cent

heaven. like all it takes is one kiss & before morning,
you could scatter his whole mind across a field.

WATCHING A FIGHT AT THE NEW HAVEN DOG PARK, FIRST TWO DOGS AND THEN THEIR OWNERS

The mailman still hands me bills like I should feel lucky to have my name on anything in this town & I been here 14 months & all I get is paper telling me who I owe & when I owe them & what might be taken from me if I don't hand over the faces of dead men & I love the electric architecture of noise on the corner of Chapel & State where the old dudes who drown their afternoons in warm liquid build porches from neon glass & yell I see you boy at the Yale kids who walk by dressed in salmon-colored windbreakers regardless of whether the wind is present or asking to be broken & I, too, dress for the hell I want & not the hell that is most likely coming & at the fence outside the dog park my own dog pulls toward home & all of my dogs pull toward home & I am a leash sometimes & I send flowers to funerals from 3 states away now & I'm saying that which forces us to bare our teeth is all a matter of perspective & inside the dog park a game of fetch has gone awry & the dog that looks like a wheat field is circling the dog that looks like a melted ice cream cone & the wheat field is all teeth & the melted cone is a trembling mess & when the stakes are most violent I suppose we all become what we resemble most & what I mean is that the men on the corner are only drunks until the cops come & then they are scholars & I am from the kind of place where no one makes a fist if they aren't going to throw the thing & when the wheat field lunges, the melted cone knows what's what & sidesteps the glistening teeth with impeccable precision & I can't believe that all of this is over a stick but I imagine that to a dog, a stick is an entire country & surely I've thrown hands in the name of less & the dogs have owners & the owners are chest to chest & yelling at each other about which dog started the fight that is a fight in name only, the wheat-field dog lunging & missing & lunging & missing & I feel guilty when I start to hope that the dog owners throw a punch at each other just so I can remember what it looks like when a fist determines its own destiny & I haven't seen a real fight since Chris from Linden mopped up some kid from the suburbs back in '02 outside of the Dairy Queen after the kid had one too many jokes about Chris's pops catching 25 years on the back of some real shit & Chris knocked that boy out so fast he ain't even get touched & we carried Chris home with his clean face & clean hands & so I really don't have the time for all of the theater at this dog park & I am getting too old & I want only a good dog most days & I'm saying I want a dog that will never ask me to finish something it started & I'm saying I want a dog that will never make me clean its blood out of the streets.

THE GHOST OF MARVIN GAYE PLAYS THE DOZENS WITH THE POP CHARTS

your mouth so wide
> it swallow a whole city in one bite

your mouth so wide
> all the black people in Detroit don't remember what they parents danced to

you think you so black
> you paint the stars on your chest

you think you so black
> you got a bed in everybody house

you take the last chicken leg
> & leave meat on the bone

you think the tea
> just got sweet from the sugar

you so ugly
> the mirror trembled at your new
>> white face & then you walked
>> into the mirror

           & then you became the mirror

              & then you tore the skin from anyone who stood before you

                  & then there was a trader joe's in the lot where we used to have the

                    block party & then everything you drank from became a whisper

your mouth so wide

      when it opens I can see myself

      crawling out starved and

      thrashing against your tongue

         an old suit hanging from my fragile

arms I have tried on all of your clothes & still nothing fits

but the blood.

everybody wanna make soul but don't nobody wanna chew a hole through the
night small enough for a bullet to pass through & pull each of their lovers into it.

everybody wanna make soul but don't nobody wanna hemorrhage a whole family
into sweat & white powder & so much sex that they will never speak of what killed you.

your mama so full she a whole planet. your mama so black she everywhere but ain't never on time. your mama so black she sang hound dog first & died with nothing to her name but the drink that carried her   to the grave. your mama so black she my mama too. your mama saw the gun & let you bleed out & ran screaming into the sunlight. your mama so black she know when there ain't nothing left worth saving. your mama so black she will come for you & know by your smell that you ain't one of her own. your mama so black she will carry you in her teeth to the river & hold you down until you become either holy or dead.

WELCOME TO HEARTBREAK

it is the version of me fading in photos that I most wish to dance with. just once before the coughing black makes a ghost of him. no one asks me to smile these days & so here is my mouth, again a straight line. border between an ocean & thirst. I thumb the edges of the picture frame & consider the wood—what tree had to fall in order for this younger & smiling version of myself to have a home. It is the killing season again. All the flowers drag the crowns of their heads along the snow & die with a prayer of softer ground on their lips. I wish this type of betrayal on no one: being born out of that which will be your undoing.

Imagine, instead: the place where you have a bed of your own & a table to sit across from someone who laughs thick & echoing as an open palm at your smallest joy & then

the fingers close

I TEND TO THINK FORGIVENESS LOOKS THE WAY IT DOES IN THE MOVIES

like two white people kissing in the rain & it is always   white people kissing in the rain on television

& it is a question of hair, I imagine. the things too precious to be given over to the illusion of

vulnerability. I have paid my tithes in this church, though. drawing my desires long through a city of

millions with wet sneakers & dying flowers exploding from tissue paper & I have emerged from this

shrinking heaven half-drowned & with a heart molding at the edges & speaking of the heart, I love

most what it is until it decides it isn't. first a weapon & then not. first a morning, wherein you see

yourself briefly

whole & next to someone else who is briefly whole & then not. I am talking about the end of love—how

the door closes one night & never reopens. The coffee mug left with a lover's unshakable stains in the

bottom & the single fork from the infant night in the first shared apartment & all of the relics we have

to craft the leash used to keep our misery close. what I meant to say about kissing in the rain is that it

seems to be about a mercy that I cannot touch, for what the water has been known to undo & what of

myself I might see in the wake of its undoing. Mercy, like the boy pulling back a fist as the small stray

dog below him trembles with its eyes shut. Mercy, that boy then walking into the arms of his mother, who once dragged him from a home ransacked by a man's violence. Mercy, the city unfolding its wide

& generous palms over your skin the way a city does when it opens itself up & darkness to pour into

its open mouth & you, too, wait for the night to spill itself into your echoing terraces of grief & call you

outside & tell you that it is almost your season, darling. it is almost the season of your favorite flower &

the burial ground giving way to its tiny & exploding lips & how they exist for you & no one else

HOW CAN BLACK PEOPLE WRITE ABOUT FLOWERS AT A TIME LIKE THIS

i have been told that in any discussion of weather, a *warning* is more severe

than a *watch*. peep the two boys on the school yard making a halo of dead

grass, their hands in the shape an elder taught them to make when describing a scar

from another violent era. no one is about that real shit until they are. in xenia, the people were warned to

watch the skies & still stayed in the fields when the clouds locked arms & began their pirouette along the

    already barren landscape. that real shit ain't about nothing until it is. after the tornado, only the witch

hazel survived. poking its tendrils up from the dirt. twisted fingers, cursing the sky. survive all manner of

cataclysm & find yourself in dark recesses, a salve for the wicked living of someone you do not know &

    are attached to nonetheless. between you & me, i was warned to watch the space where the fissure

    began & still, I filled my mouth with cake. enjoy the sweetness now, before it comes back to claim

    a space that you'd rather keep hidden. the difference between a warning & a threat is all a matter of

    what you've lived through. watch the fist sew shut the eye of a boy who was warned about talking

    slick. watch the thin

tentacles of blood surround the fresh damage. the only surviving instrument.

IT'S NOT LIKE NIKOLA TESLA KNEW ALL OF THOSE PEOPLE WERE GOING TO DIE

Everyone wants to write about god
but no one wants to imagine their god

as the finger trembling inside a grenade
pin's ring or the red vine of blood coughed into a child's palm

while they cradle the head of a dying parent.
Few things are more dangerous than a man

who is capable of dividing himself into several men,
each of them with a unique river of desire

on their tongue. It is also magic to pray for a daughter
and find yourself with an endless march of boys

who all have the smile of a motherfucker who wronged you
and never apologized. No one wants to imagine their god

as the knuckles cracking on a father watching his son
picking a good switch from the tree and certainly

no one wants to imagine their god as the tree.
Enough with the foolishness of hope and how it bruises

the walls of a home where two people sit, stubbornly in love
with the idea of staying. If one must pray, I imagine

it is most worthwhile to pray toward endings.
The only difference between sunsets and funerals

is whether or not a town mistakes the howls
of a crying woman for madness.

YOU ABOUT TO TELL HER YOU LOVE HER, WE OFF THAT

I text you & instead say *distance is a mirror inside*
of which the only echo is your face but then I delete
it & I type something to make you think I laughed
at the joke / the one about a dog / the one about

a boy / the one about making your own ending &
walking through it & I thought of you during the movie
in the dark of the theater when the man had a gun pointed
at his head & he closed his eyes & prayed as if god has any

sway over the evil unlocked in a stranger's hands & I thought
of you on the way home when the car was being pushed
through the gap of snow by 5 people & still moving only
inches & I think of you now when the blades of a helicopter sever

the single cloud & it becomes two drifting corpses, one for each
coast & the thing about texting a joke is that no one cares whether
it's actually funny & when we are not in the same room
I imagine a lie to be better than silence & the word *hollow*

in any language sounds like something the body wants no part
of & I text you again: *I have made my own ending & the door is yawning*
& on the other side of it I am praying & I am pushing & I am drifting away
& the funny thing about the boy who cries wolf is that he eventually becomes one

ONE SIDE OF AN INTERVIEW WITH THE GHOST OF MARVIN GAYE

after Eve L. Ewing

A: yes. he was a preacher.

A: you let a man see god once and he'll learn to make a country out of anything.

A: I think what I'm saying is that I prayed to any sound I could tempt out of a body.

A: hunger is whatever shape the moonlight pulls your shadow into.

A: yes. I served as many masters as it took.

A: it wasn't only sex, but people hear what they want when the world is on fire.

A: smoke said once you make people believe that you got something they need, you can make them believe anything.

A: yes, I grew tired of waiting on my grave, so I seduced one out of thin air.

A: commandments? at least 8.

A: the joke was that to be sanctified, you gotta set a distance between yourself and what you love.

A: no. I never got to ask for her forgiveness.

A: no. She never came back.

A: that's the thing about being empty I guess.

A: everyone who thinks of death as a peaceful place is still alive

WITH BOXES PILED AT THE FOOT OF THE STAIRS, I GO TO SEE LOGAN

I will not spoil
the ending, though

what is there to spoil
but to say there was

a casket in the place
you would imagine

a casket to be.
depending on how

you define burial,
the ending is unspectacular.

my pal died not when the pill bottle
rolled empty from his unfurling

palm. it was sometime after
that, when I told his old girlfriend

I have maybe been in love
with you the whole time.

HOW CAN BLACK PEOPLE WRITE ABOUT FLOWERS AT A TIME LIKE THIS

Kehinde painted

that man Barack

with roses at his feet

the saying goes

get your roses

while you're still alive

to smell them

show me a way to govern

without violence

and I will show you

a way to not feel

shame inside

of the moment

when a person recognizes

their face

in the face of their captor

and falls in love

with the familiarity

I too have licked

the blood from a mirror

in an attempt

to see more clearly

the lips thick

        with a familiar slang

flooding the tongue

        get me to the curve

of a lover's neck

        while I am still alive enough

for my nose

        to resist disappearing

my blessings into ash

        depending on what is in bloom

I might summon

the blade

I might undo

the forest winding

its way along

the sides of my face

so that I can

more closely resemble

a man worthy

of waking to roses

at his feet

in a kill or be killed

nation

          give to my open palms

   something that

      might die before I do

until all that remain

        are the thorns

   pushing their lips

      together and begging

for touch.

IT IS MAYBE TIME TO ADMIT THAT MICHAEL JORDAN DEFINITELY PUSHED OFF

that one time in the '98 NBA finals & in praise of one man's hand on the waist of another & in praise of the ways we guide our ships to the shore of some brief & gilded mercy I touch my fingers to the hips of this vast & immovable grief & push once more & who is to say really how much weight was behind Jordan's palm on that night in Utah & on that same night one year earlier the paramedics pulled my drowning mother from the sheets where she slept & they said it must have felt like a whole hand was pushing down on her lungs & I spent the whole summer holding my breath in bed until the small black spots danced on the ceiling & I am sorry that there is no way to describe this that is not about agony or that is not about someone being torn from the perch of their comfort & on the same night a year before my mother died Jordan wept on the floor of the United Center locker room after winning another title because it was father's day & his father went to sleep on the side of a road in '93 & woke up a ghost & there is no moment worth falling to our knees & galloping toward like the one that sings our dead into the architecture & so yes for a moment in 1998 Michael Jordan made what space he could on the path between him & his father's small & breathing grace

& so yes,

there is an ocean between us the length of my arm & I have built nothing for you that can survive it

& from here I am close enough to be seen but not close enough to be cherished

& from here, I can see every possible ending before we even touch.

GLAMOUR ON THE WEST STREETS / SILVER OVER EVERYTHING

from the humid brick building below my humid brick building, a woman
bellows at the pizza man. who, it seems, threw no cheese atop the crust
& its red river of sauce because—as he shouts above the sirens of State
Street & the growing crowd lined outside his shop—it is Friday night
& he is woefully short on mozzarella & there are far better pizza options
on every corner of this city, overpriced & tonight bursting at the seams
with lonely people who will seek the warmth spilling from the edges
of a cardboard box & onto their laps & into their fingers on the walk
back to a newly empty apartment. I love the heat for how it separates
the desire for touch from the practicality of it. If it gets too hot to fuck,
as it did for mookie & tina, then we're all on our own sinking islands
anyway. there is no cheese in this town anymore & what could be worse
than the fraction of a dream behind every door you crawl to. it is friday & surely
some of my people are praising the fresh coin in their bank accounts & what
a tragedy to spend it on a half-finished freedom & the argument below has poured
out into the streets & the waiting masses & I imagine this is no longer over
cheese but over every mode of unfulfilled promise. the cluster of sins still stuck to a body
fresh from the waters of baptism. the parent who must dig a grave for their youngest
child. from below, a man yells *there are only three ingredients. you can't even get that right.*
isn't it funny, to vow that you will love someone until you are dead.

THE GHOST OF MARVIN GAYE STANDS OVER HIS FATHER'S GRAVE AND FORGETS TO ASK FOR AN APOLOGY

They ain't make a religion yet that lets you trade in mercy for more sins. Can you believe the boys these days? They open their mouth & a machine holds their voice. In a balled fist. They ain't even dancing no more, pop. There ain't nothing out there for someone lonely to look at & dream about in a corner of a cold bed. I told 'em you left all those bruises so that you could always have a map to me, father. I told 'em the belt buckle's echo along a brick wall was how I learned the charity of silence. Look at me now. All I got to call my own is quiet. Ain't no forgiveness for men like us. Ain't no god in any architecture where we goin'. Only thing that separates purgatory and hell is whether or not you can see the face of someone you've loved in the fire, baby, and I'm good with what I ain't got. Wouldn't know what to do if I could look myself in the eye. Thank you for opening the door to this eternity. I wasn't gonna be out here digging a hole for any child I brought into this world. I wasn't ever trynna bury nothin' but my own self. I sang that shit that could get somebody free. The women all threw roses at my feet in California until the roses looked like chains.

AND JUST LIKE THAT, I PART WAYS WITH THE ONLY THING I WON IN THE DIVORCE

one night with some dive's secondhand smoke playing a love song

above our heads & our fingers slicked with grease from someone's fried

chicken, amy said *afrofuturism is simply the idea that black people will exist*

in the future & i watched the fullness of the malt liquor bottle jump

its way to empty at the tilt of an old head's lips & i said *i am not so sure*

& like any self-fashioned god, i cherry-pick the aesthetics of my own resurrection.

the salesman wants to talk to me about leather & how it is ethically made

because the hide of the dead animal would be destroyed anyway & so you see,

even something discarded deserves a second life & in praise of this, i dig

my fingers into the seat of the new car with one hand & find a tune

with the other & i spent 3 seasons cutting off the parts of myself destined

for destruction & yet no one has fashioned them into anything useful &

i mean to look the old heads in the eye & say *i wish you wouldn't smoke*

that shit 'round me but instead i say *take into yourself that which might get you closer*

to heaven and blow some over my head. who wants the burden of being an ancestor

anyway, i tell the salesman who has two children & another on the way.

a crown made of assassin's tools is still a crown. i have enough money

in my pocket to buy my way out of the relics of grief & i don't say this

lightly. pay me what you owe me for the way my heart breaking has made yours

feel less like an anchor & in exchange, i will tell you that true wealth

is the ability to embrace forgetting. to my children, i will leave only the ways

i didn't let them down, written on small pieces of paper & hidden amid

a graveyard of animal hides. for now, i say i will take the one with the sun-
roof. i want this particular wind all to myself. i want it to blow through
the absence of hair & know there would have been a passenger there once.
i want to hear it, through clenched teeth, hissing *i've had enough of you now.*

HOW CAN BLACK PEOPLE WRITE ABOUT FLOWERS AT A TIME LIKE THIS

with my eyes closed long enough,
i can at least remember the popping
of gum thrashing between Jasmine's
teeth. i would like for memory alone
to declare me forgiven but i would be lying
if i said i recall the color of the dress
or the way her hair spread its many arms
along the blacktop. i nurse whatever visions
i must for the sake of enduring. of course,
i tell myself it was the popping of gum.
of course, i say that she was pulled to the ground
by revelry, and nothing else. of course, i
do not ask you to relive with me the funeral,
though by now you surely know there was one.

THE OLD HEAD GIVES BAD ADVICE WHILE A MAN SITS WITH A GUN

on his lap in a white suv dragging down the santa ana freeway encased by a parade of blue & whites
with their sirens on mute & still flashing & running their claws along the exterior of the whip & nbc
cut the nba finals off for this & in ohio my pops would let the brooklyn leap out his voice whenever
the knicks were winning & ewing had hakeem grasping at ghosts that night like my man angelo who
hadn't slept in a month since the echo of a night's pistol replaced his sister in the gospel choir & mario
said that if we wanted to watch a black man run from the cops we could just go down to livingston ave
on the 1st or 15th & so we grabbed the rock & ran toward the orange halo cutting through the starless
black & painted the sky with our sweat & shouting & the rim's vibration from our misses & we backed
off josh at the 3-point line cuz he missed everything & rule is you crowd the shooter whether or not
you think they might actually shoot & some would say that as everyone is capable of dying everyone is
capable of killing or everyone is capable of the fear that sends a hand reaching for a killing instrument
& that night the heat lapped at our hand-me-down shirts as we ran home & the heat sat on the lap of
a man running home to his mother & enough love cannot bleach the blood from your hands but that
won't stop the men from trying & past the porch on barnett the old man sat with his radio & his beer
& the glow of a tv & the white suv still making its crawl home towards absolution & the man looked
us up and down & thumbed the picture of his wife from the day they were married & through the
window his bed was made up & hadn't been slept in for at least a month & he stared at the suv splitting
the los angeles sunlight & said *don't you boys ever fall in love*

THE TURN

Drowning people
Sometimes die
Fighting their rescuers
—OCTAVIA BUTLER

I WOULD ASK YOU TO RECONSIDER THE IDEA THAT THINGS ARE AS BAD AS THEY'VE EVER BEEN

In the year that felt like one
hundred years, Kendrick let
a small flame dance along the tight
braids pulled in rows along his head

by someone with thin & aching
fingers & when two trains sped
along the tracks outside
of our emptying apartment,

either swallowed by a sprawling city
or being coughed out of it,
the windows shook & one night
the picture of a man—

who was supposed to be Jesus
but looked like no savior
the hood would ever claim—
fell off the bookcase

& in the morning, I stepped
in the broken frame's constellation
of glass & it might seem like
what I'm saying is that hell always comes

from above & seduces its way
south but what I am *really* saying
is the true daughter of desolation
is that which finds a home

inside of you when nothing else
will. the thing that burrows
& makes a way even
beyond the bone & I am fed up,

again, with the prediction
of my own misery.
Art imitates life, but particularly
the moment where flesh was broken

into once & then somehow
found a way to heal itself
again despite the body
imagining pain as a thing

of its most brutal nightmares
& I have no living mother
to call out to & so surely
you all will do for an hour,

or a night, or however long it takes
to pull from my memory
the magnifying glass
& the ants laboring beneath it

in the summer of my mother's funeral.
A boy sets insects on fire first
& then walks from a home's charred ruins
smelling of ash. A boy forgets

how he can feel pain first
& then shovels broken glass
into his mouth
with his bare hands

& the blood runs
from his lips & each drop
becomes a cardinal,
state bird of every place

where he misses someone.
O Jesus of a beard
that looks like my father's beard,
Jesus of gold chains

& a tall white tee,
Jesus of braids, rowed back
along the scalp by a thin-fingered
& long-nailed sage:

grant me the mercy
of a bed in which
I do not tangle my limbs
with anyone else's.

Grant me a cardinal that sees
its reflection in the window
of my bedroom & tries to break
the glass into one hundred pieces.

HOW CAN BLACK PEOPLE WRITE ABOUT FLOWERS AT A TIME LIKE THIS

maybe all the blues

requires is a door

through which a person

can enter and exit.

every god hides their eyes

behind a blue hood.

the hooded devil waiting

at the crossroads

doesn't give a fuck

about the women

who sent a man wailing

with a guitar case on his back.

it isn't loneliness if enough tongues

have your chorus jumping

from underneath their hooded

ruckus. maybe all the blues requires

is a person who has been touched

before & a caravan of hands

busy with their own pleasures.

if you can't fashion a song

out of that, there is no god

or devil that could make something

of your soul anyway. a father stands

over his crying son & hisses

I'll give you something to cry about

as if he didn't already

bring a child into a world

that requires neither of them.

FOR THE DOGS WHO BARKED AT ME ON THE SIDEWALKS IN CONNECTICUT

Darlings if your owners say you are / *not usually like this* / then I must take them / at their word / I am like you / not crazy about that which towers before me / particularly the buildings here / and the people inside / who look at my name / and make noises / that seem like growling / my small and eager darlings / what it must be like / to have the sound for love / and the sound for fear be a matter of pitch / I am afraid to touch / anyone who might stay / long enough to make leaving / an echo / there is a difference / between burying a thing you love / for the sake of returning / and leaving a fresh absence / in a city's dirt / looking for a mercy / left by someone / who came before you / I am saying that I / too / am at a loss for language / can't beg myself / a doorway / out of anyone / I am not usually like this either / I must apologize again for how adulthood has rendered me / us, really / I know you all forget the touch / of someone who loves you / in two minutes / and I arrive to you / a constellation of shadows / once hands / listen darlings / there is a sky / to be pulled down / into our bowls / there is a sweetness for us / to push our faces into / I promise / I will not beg for you to stay this time / I will leave you to your wild galloping / I am sorry / to hold you again / for so long / I am in the mood / to be forgotten.

HOW CAN BLACK PEOPLE WRITE ABOUT FLOWERS AT A TIME LIKE THIS

drake said *y'all better not come to my funeral*
with that fake shit. & this is how i knew

he'd never slept on a floor by way of his loneliness
& empty pockets. what is neither here nor there

is that i cling to the past because in it, i had yet to know pain
& therefore i was held only by that which desired my boyish

appetite. we buried tyler & the violets i placed on his grave
were plastic & cost 4.99 at the corner store by the punk house

where we had cake on his 19th birthday & there were purple heart-
shaped petals iced into the corner of it & i am saying that i would not know

a real violet if i ran my hands across what i imagine is its silk jaw.
i would not know, even if you pulled a string of them from your pocket

& gently planted the string along my neck & said *someone not here thought this*
would look pretty on you. friends, the trick to this one is that i laid the plastic on the grave

that i least wanted to dig. death itself, *that fake shit*
i stay praying to show up somewhere.

NONE OF MY VICES ARE VIOLENT ENOUGH TO UNDO REMEMBERING

and it is troubling isn't it
to have a reflection

that always arrives
when called despite
the steam pulling

its thick tongue
along a mirror's edges
after I emerge unsanctified

from underneath
the raging showerhead
and it is really something

to love only the unseen
and still be finite
back in the golden era

a good bluesman
would have a memory
only as long as it took

for the last guitar note
to drown itself
in something that burned

the throat on the dance down
and I guess
that doesn't

seem so bad
when you consider
the times

what I'm saying is
that if you're going to die
broke you might as well

also do it alone
my great-great-grandfather
could not swim

he played guitar
for coins on the juke circuit
but never parted his lips

for the drink
and so when the yawning maw
of the Mississippi coughed out

his remains there was no other
excuse for what dragged him
to the water

except for that which he didn't
do himself the mercy of forgetting
and in all of the pictures

I have his smile
it is dark outside my window
and I see my reflection

in everything I see
my reflection in the water
yes especially the water

THE GHOST OF MARVIN GAYE SITS IN THE RUINS OF THE OLD LIVINGSTON FLEA MARKET AND CONSIDERS MONOGAMY

there is no corner   of midnight   where I ain't   a god to somebody   & no one claps

at all the tongue's   miracles but   my daddy had a pistol & knew how   to beckon a moan

from its door   with a bent   finger & boy   all the men   I come from

could hunt & we all got   our methods   mine is bloodred   suits & sweat

in between   piano keys   & a scream   that could rock loose anyone's chains

& there ain't   no word   for this: a murder in reverse   pulling the bullet

out slow & letting   it dance   in the sheets   I'm sayin' they was   already dead

by the time I got   in the room   I'm sayin'   I most cherish how the headboard

whispers under   the right   rhythm   how it sounds like two ropes

lowering a fresh   casket into another   dark & wet   mouth

HOW CAN BLACK PEOPLE WRITE ABOUT FLOWERS AT A TIME LIKE THIS

free love till the check comes & me & mine reach in our fruitless pockets

for the wallets we know we left at the crib next to the framed black & whites

of our divorced or widowed parents. there were hand-drawn daisies on the de la

soul album cover once & now I stay on that hippie shit, arms open the length of a day's

eye & no one running toward them but an estate of ghosts—hand drawn

from the depths of memory all my worst enemies keep. native tongue & all that means

is I know the exact ground to which my moans owe their treacherous birth.

I know which branch of a tree will bend under a storm's weight & offer its palms

to my begging mouth. the satisfaction in breaking a loosely-cooked egg is in the yellow

clawing its way beyond a bondage of white. there is nothing more arrogant than beauty

at rest. de la said *D.A.I.S.Y.* meant *da inner sound, y'all* & I guess that explains the insomnia.

y'all, da inner sound is the long silence between a door slamming & the kiss of a lock, which says

you will never again in your life. put that on everything. put that on the book I slid under a table

leg to stop my yolk from running. put that on any room so empty, every name inside is an echo.

I TEND TO THINK FORGIVENESS LOOKS THE WAY IT DOES IN THE MOVIES

like in the field

       slow motion

  the grass dying

underfoot

       someone turns

  to face back

       right at the last minute

before the train leaves

       the sun sets

  all is forgiven

the flood returns

hungry and merciless and without words

speaking of words

I tell my therapist

you can't spell

heartbreak without art

and she doesn't laugh

but it's true look

at how I whip my arms

in the empty apartment again

to the song

from the movie

where someone walked back

     through the door

        they once walked out of

look at how I keep

     playing the b sides and skipping the hits

look at how I build a shrine

        to afterthoughts

    I know *this* isn't therapy

I know that we aren't even

       friends but tell me what it meant

    when as a boy

I sat at the mouth

of the gumball machines

with no quarters

in my pockets

twisting each metal diamond

and hoping for a miracle

tell me what it meant

that when the first ball dropped

my hands were not ready

and I watched it roll in slow

motion down the mall floor

until another child more eager

than I was parted

their palms like they were catching

the last living dove

tell me what it meant

that I did not weep when the child

pushed the gumball between their teeth

with their eyes on me

the entire time

tell me what it means now

that one cannot say *heartbreak*

without the lips

making a soft circle of themselves

at the opening of *break*

as they also might to beckon a kiss

is it that memory is a field

with endless graves

IT'S NOT LIKE NIKOLA TESLA KNEW ALL OF THOSE PEOPLE WERE GOING TO DIE

It is impossible to tell your saints from your sinners when a fistful of dollar bills descends on a room. It is usually a question of who is willing to go home with less blood than they brought to the party. Some of us work for our meals, and some of us eat the dead pulled from the top hat of a hunter. What I'm saying is that after I crawled out of the pit, I knew the blood on my shirt was not a child of any wound I owned, but I still wore it the way fire wears a city it is only a visitor in. If the trick is not knowing whom to trust, how am I to stop myself from turning my heart over to a man who disappears and then reappears somewhere else with the weight of fresh coins burdening his pockets? When me and my boys filled our backpacks with handfuls of candy from the shelves at CVS and walked out underneath the cashier's stern gaze, I imagine a field of rabbits pushed their heads out of the black soil somewhere east of where the cops beat Big Mike's ass against the metal fence at Johnson Park when he came back to the hood with enough money in his pocket to buy his mama a crib big enough to hold a proper wake. It might seem like I am preparing you for another vanishing act, but that's not the trick either. It's not like I can promise the return of anyone but myself, and then where would that leave you? Loneliness is the drug from which all other drugs obtain their architecture. But maybe I don't mean *loneliness* as much as I mean isolation. Maybe I mean having someone waiting for you in a bed while you sit in a running car and trace another person's name into the fogged window with your smallest finger. Father, forgive us, for we know exactly what we do. Father, forgive us, for we were dragged by our collars to the cliffs, where we watched the lightning's jagged spine open and split a tree, which fell on a house where there might have been a sleeping family. Forgive us, for we saw what your worst intentions were capable of and tried to catch them in our hands anyway.

HOW CAN BLACK PEOPLE WRITE ABOUT FLOWERS AT A TIME LIKE THIS

but if you'll indulge / my worst impulses / isn't it funny / how the white / petals of the oleander / do not render the crow / flightless / upon being swallowed / and yet / the human body / crumbles under the weight / of their softness / by *funny* / you may think the joke / is about the black / thing consuming a bouquet of white / ness / without falling / from the sky / in droves / but by *funny* I mean / I am adorning my fingertips / with white petals / and running a thumb / along the edges / of your mouth / agape with a rapturous / desire / to hoard desire is one way / of becoming a fiend / my homie / peddled white / to fiends who / took the white / peddled / into themselves / and some / did not survive / but some / I imagine / grew brief / black wings / having never felt it / I will still wish upon you / the feeling of knowing / exactly where your next high / will be born from / I do not define / the distance between sinning / and deliverance / I pedaled the white / bike / downtown / on a Tuesday / the homie got 15 / for hoarding the white / he had yet to peddle / inside of a suitcase / his mother cried / inside of the courtroom / mad / perhaps / with the sudden descent / of feathers

IF LIFE IS AS SHORT AS OUR ANCESTORS INSIST IT IS, WHY ISN'T EVERYTHING I WANT ALREADY AT MY FEET

if I make it to heaven, I will ask for all of the small pleasures I could have had on earth.
And I'm sure this will upset the divine order. I am a simple man.

I want, mostly, a year that will not kill me when it is over.
A hot stove and a wooden porch bent under the weight of my people.

I was born, and it only got worse from there.
In the dead chill of a doctor's office, I am told what to cut

back on and what to add more of. None of this sounds like living.
I sit in a running car under a bath of orange light and eat

the fried chicken that I swore an oath to stray from
for the sake of my heart and its blood labor.

Still, there is something about the way a grease stain begins small and then tiptoes
its way along the fabric of my pants. Here, finally, a country worth living in.

One that falls thick from whatever it is we love so much
that we can't stop letting it kill us. If we must die, let it be inside here. If we must.

THE GHOST OF MARVIN GAYE PUTS A SEASHELL TO HIS EAR AND HEARS A MOAN FROM THE LAST WOMAN HE LOVED

Funny how they ain't teach us how to unwrite a song
once it pulls the twilight down and makes a mess

of the tangled limbs. My skin, a different kind of blue
than the one that gave birth to my American lineage.

My skin, under the spotlight of any stage,
is what made me less hunter and more prey. I understand

the language of wetness. The way sound searches for a mother
—as we all do once we are coughed into the ache

of a dry and loveless interior. What some called hallucination
I called a sunrise. A morning with another set of legs

to free myself from. And they ain't teach that either. That was all me. None
of the shit people say feels like drowning
actually does.

MAN IT'S SO HARD NOT TO ACT RECKLESS

You cannot serve / two masters / unless they both crave / the same riches / I serve every master / who arrives empty / to my door / I guess I should've forgotten / where I came / from / all of my idols died / because they took too much / of something into themselves / must be the pharaohs / niggas ain't make it out the hood / to be buried with only / the dirt / they came out of / heaven's gate / is a suicide door / my mama couldn't get through / get fly to get fly / darkness swallowing the afternoon / and still / no one to go home with tonight / except the shadows & / some have teeth / how he stay faithful / in a room / full of ghosts / I am double parked / sideways / outside the collapse / of a country & / didn't nobody here / fuck with me / ever since my name / became my name / & now I'm too bad / to be governed / by anything sent / from the tip of any devil's / finger / I'm serious / nigga / I'm talking like / it's just me / it's just the mirror / & a day where I am loved / by no one / & if not for our small / rituals / how would we get out / of the house / the question I ask / of the sun slouching / its way in / through the gapped / teeth of morning / is what of myself / I have to sew back / together / in order to face / the aching & vanishing landscape / ain't a bank account / big enough / for the particular nightmare / in which the world ends / except for the corner of it / where you live / with the person you stopped loving / wait till I get my / money / wait till I get / my nothing / right / I couldn't tell you / who decides wars.

HOW CAN BLACK PEOPLE WRITE ABOUT FLOWERS AT A TIME LIKE THIS

when i tell him about the threat at my doorstep,

the childhood homie thumbs the blue lip

of his waistband & says *these niggas don't want no smoke*

& i suppose that is true, though i do recall

the wooden underbelly of the incense holder

 & how, before it began to fade, it was adorned

with orchids, which were carved into it by hand

& it was carried across an ocean by someone a man loved

enough to call *brother* despite their sharing no history beyond their necks

craned over the Quran & the women who wanted

so desperately for them to come to bed.

it is impossible to name the blood leashed to your own until you,

like the orchid, fold into anything outside with skin

close enough to yours & sprout a newer & more violent

body. it is impossible to know what you'd kill

for until you hold a face in your two hands

underneath a streetlight on a block where killing pays

the rent. where, as a boy, i would pluck the incense

from its plastic & place it in the tight ring

of the incense holder's mouth & my father would sing

the call to prayer while the white smoke plumed & divided

into siblings with each syllable & so i think it is true

that *niggas don't want no smoke* if by that i am saying niggas

don't want to be a memory or niggas don't want to have their name blown

from their father's lips in a prayer of forgetting. i tell the homie

not to bring guns to my resting place. someone i love is sleeping here tonight.

& i remember us as young, his mother in a hospital bed holding both of our faces & saying

you boys have to remember to always take care of each other.

IT OCCURS TO ME THAT I AM LOVED MOST FOR THE THINGS I REFUSE

to do out of anger / or lust / or whatever keeps me up at night / what I like most / about rage / is that it moves / an animal / of the body's own / fashioning / the leash on mine / is so fly / it makes the animal itself / invisible / in the religion / I found myself born into / and then tasked with / restraint was a currency / I imagine this / is why my therapist / knows where / her next meal / is coming from / you are what you / don't / eat / is the joke I tell / while I push the bacon / to the side of the plate / and this is all / I have in common / with my father / I am most romantic / when I let a fist fall / limp at my side / I'm still yelling / put some respect / on whatever my name sounds like / out of the mouths / of your white friends / put some respect on the hood / in which I am a target / put a thick gold chain on the neck / of the statue I am building / for the man who worked / shining shoes / for forty years / kneeling for people / who tossed him coins / without speaking / put some coins in the fountain / that the statue will rest in / immovability is a type of reparations / the inspirational speaker asks us to imagine / that we can become anything / I ask him to imagine that anything / can become us.

THE PRESTIGE

The thing about not watching my mother get old is that I wasn't never sure what I was gonna get, cause if you don't got yr folks to look at, if all you got to look at is a picture of a woman standing beside a cactus, a picture took by a man who weren't ever really your daddy, then you don't got a good idea really of where yr headed. When I seen her bones I knew what we all knew, that we's all gonna end up in a grave someday, but there's stops in between there and now.

—SUZAN-LORI PARKS

LIGHTS OUT TONIGHT, TROUBLE IN THE HEARTLAND

and besides, by the time this ends, you will have forgotten what drew you here in the first place.

the volta here is the prey, standing in the stomach of a hollow cavern with a dying predator

in its mouth. the way I showed up to the basketball court on scottwood with the blood of my

grade-school tormenter adorning my white kicks, and then went a year without having to make

a fist. I hear violence is unbecoming, but in the moment it is all I have to throw over both of our

shoulders. In the teeth of my beloved, I am being dragged, coughing, to the center of a field

that sprouts my mother's favorite flower. Each of them comes out of the ground dying.

Do you get it now? No matter how beautiful a child illustrates it, the actual heart is an ugly machine.

A hideous chorus of chambers. It gets what it deserves.

NO DIGGITY

Shorty get / down / good lord / and yes the lord / is good / the lord is / as lonely / as I feel / in the darkness / of a strange city / and the lord / points / me to the light / I say twice on Sunday / and mean I see a savior / in everyone / my niggas say we come / from kings / and they mean / our fathers / have blood / on their hands / they mean / someone had to die / for the money in our pockets / money which tonight / is fanned out / like the wings of a hunting / falcon / across the face / of a counter / at a fried-chicken joint / where they serve / what our mothers taught us / how to cook in their kitchens / what our mothers learned / from their mothers / and their mothers before them / and so we are here / in honor of the first / black / woman / to drop anything / in hot oil / in honor of the first / black / woman / to prepare a feast / for a family / while her own children / held their aching / and hollow stomachs / in honor of this / I will be fed / by someone else's hands / tonight / I will laugh at the bad / joke / I will say *make love* / and mean the sound / an open palm makes / when it slaps a table / while holding a card / and the fate of an entire / night's humor / everyone I roll with / is not above taking / into ourselves / that which will one day / kill us / something fried / to praise / in the name of our small / and generous lords / I say twice on Sunday / and mean I stay one foot / in the grave / with the flyest / kicks on / I mean / I'm back on my bullshit / I'm back in my feelings / again / and I think / I'm going to stay / this time / everything I miss / is a monument / I cannot see through / and yet / a small child / smiles at me / from over / their mother's back / and I name the child / after all of you / I build them a small / future / and listen / if I am being honest / I am weary tonight / of giving the bullet / more space than the living / tonight I want a meal / I could have made / in my own kitchen / with my mother's arms / over my shoulders / tonight I want no love / that doesn't crumble / and stain every part of me / it echoes through / tonight / I will watch the stars rust / in the arms of no one / turns out / daylight is the new / misery / and I am drowning / I am drowning / I am drowning / party's over boys / where we going / for breakfast

THE GHOST OF MARVIN GAYE MISTAKES A RECORD STORE FOR A GRAVEYARD

they burned the disco records

                and from the smoke I heard

my mother's voice or was it

                that my father once wore

my mother's dresses spun in front of a mirror

                the music he tried to pray out of himself

memory is as fleeting as any other high

                never tell anyone you love them

with the lights off or with a halo of lipstick

                around the edges of a bedsheet

staining the gospel

or was it that my father simply loved

when my mother pushed a boy out to be given

his name in every reflection of myself

a father's violence gaping

when the women called to me

in any bedroom

the walls opened up bullet holes

like the small mouths of boys

trying to sing along to hymns

on Saturday mornings from the corners

of their mother's best dress it is funny

how even a trick of the ears can turn   hearing a weapon

a night in London they yelled

                              marvin / marvin / marvin

and I saw devils hanging

                                        at the end of every curtain

NONE OF MY BLACK FRIENDS WANT TO LISTEN TO DON'T STOP BELIEVIN'

but we all know what it is when the *street / light* comes on

& I don't mean to romanticize darkness but I do perhaps mean to say

I want to dance in the moments before the sunset lets me out

of its clutches & fear carves a crib into the pit

of some mother's stomach. The news says that soon

it's going to feel like summer all year & then what

will we make of winter & the way nighttime gallops in

before our bodies are ready to lie down with each other

& I know. I hear you thinking *there he goes again.*

But let me promise you that this time it really is just about a song

& the coins rattling in my pocket & the way they beg to be pushed

into a jukebox when the sky is a color that demands singing

& nothing else. But if you will indulge me—since you are

still here—I will say the words

hold on to that feeling & the wind might blow the shadow

of someone you miss through your outstretched fingers.

I don't know anymore what it is we are all reaching for, but here

we are & somewhere along the line we learned the difference

between the gospel that will keep us out of hell & the shit they play

to wake up the polo shirts in suburban pews & I say *we* & you already know

I mean those of us who have reached for a song & pulled back a coffin

& *we* don't sing our gospel in bars. *We* don't sing where we sin.

We don't lock arms and wake up a hood that ain't ours,

where they call the cops if a leaf rattles outside a window past midnight

& this is why I hang back under the flickering *street / light*

& listen to the hum of rusting air conditioners buzzing in late November

& maybe all the songs we don't want to sing out loud anymore

are about someone on a porch, wringing their hands together

& hoping a person who shares their blood cuts

through the night & walks into their arms.

HOW CAN BLACK PEOPLE WRITE ABOUT FLOWERS AT A TIME LIKE THIS

& it turns out

        lineage is the most
        vicious stunt of them all

name me after the first
hands to shake the dirt

           off my arms & lay diamonds
           on my wrist or name me after the pistol

kept in the nightstand of a free
man who wasn't afraid to use it

           you get what I'm saying
           name me for the bride

I crane my neck toward
each time she runs the pitch-

           black gospel choir back into town
           imperial in my stunt gold

all in my mouth
so I talk that shit

      them white folk shook the hills down
      for & now they can't keep my seeds

out the air or earth
& even the hollow shells

      of them can close a throat
      before it starts to play me for a fool

look I'm crowning so wide
I got enough shade to feed ten summers

      & ten porches of women fanning
      themselves with the old testament

& leaning in for the good gossip
& whispering *don't you know there are whole*

      fields on fire still & I take my reparations
      in the almost fading blond petals twirling off the black

stem like when nina sang pirate jenny

& the song became about a slave ship

name me after the last nigga

who held the apocalypse in their palms

& rocked it to sleep

for long enough to throw

one more drink on the tab

or the first nigga to have an address everywhere

but one rent check

I'm too fly to haunt anything

but my own reflection &

so when I'm gone I'm gone &

the most vicious stunt of all is how this was your language first

IT'S NOT LIKE NIKOLA TESLA KNEW ALL OF THOSE PEOPLE WERE GOING TO DIE

if man is not supposed to play

God then

why did God make dying look

so beautiful.

I guess there were no bullets

& so the nails

had to suffice & in defense

of lightning

there is always a darkness

asking to be

split open. as a boy, I saw an

electric tongue

dance along the oak tree

outside my window

& the two halves held

themselves together

by three wooden threads

for years & I grew

to imagine them as hands

nailed to each

other & I may have once

whispered *I want*

a love like that into the empty
space—severed but
forgiving. don't you know
they bury men
like me alive with all of our
sentimental longing.
Tesla said *there are no great*
inventions made by
married men but then how
do you explain
the way the space in between
bodies in a shared
bed can feel like an entire
country? I'm saying
that all inventions come
at the cost of a room
becoming something
different than it was.
a boy who imagines himself
alone falls from an abandoned
skyscraper & halves the sky
& there is nothing up there

that will hold any of us
together & darling I think
I've got it—I can tell
Magic from science by
whether or not
there is a body
in the casket.

WHAT A MIRACLE THAT OUR PARENTS HAD US WHEN THEY COULD HAVE GOTTEN A PUPPY INSTEAD

i guess it is good to know you are needed by something that won't outgrow you. or that won't learn a name to call you outside of. i am back to wearing sweaters in summer. it's a question of intimacy. that which will do the work of love for those who have grown weary of loving me. every four years in america it becomes fashionable to make promises you can't keep and so here i am again. i tell you that i will try to make it to your brunch/reading/karaoke night and then i draw a blanket over my chest and look to see who will deliver me something warm. i hold a face in my palms and turn it toward a field of sunflowers, their bright ridges arched into the night's humid mouth. i say *i will always be here, as i am now* and the true lie is that time doesn't already have its talons in all of our backs, pulling a younger version of ourselves thrashing to the gates after each passing hour. i am lying, too, about my dog and what the years have done to her. i am lying about this though I see the way she eyes the flight of steps at the entrance to our home. she makes it up them, yes, but then gasps over a water bowl. nothing is like it was in the old days, they say. everything outside is dying easier. melting. the answer to thirst as our undoing. i take up whatever space i must and apologize later. in the mirror, i am already vanishing. it's the need to be loved that we'll all miss most. my dog doesn't always run when i call her name. i don't always reply to my father's texts.

WOMEN AND CHILDREN FIRST AND THE CHILDREN FIRST AND THE CHILDREN

are still dying   somewhere not here the man on television   wears a tie the color of a fresh   sky
unburdened   by the machines of war   and I think it is warm this year I think I loved you best
when warmth   was something to be hoarded between limbs (ice age coming /   ice age coming /
let me hear /   both sides) ok: I have made room   for joy though

the oceans   may not allow my children's children to see room for joy & isn't that the way? I toss my dice
        against the immovable   future & only bad numbers   come back &   yet (take the money / and
run / take the money /   and run / take the money) here,   I'm alive & standing

in summer's   unbearable yawn   & for the purpose   of romantics in the face of extinction   I say
sweat now   & mean disintegration I say sweat & mean I am melting   like everything else but this
is a parting   gift the way I become water   another vessel for you to find your   reflection in & may
I go first   before everyone   I love & I am once   again demanding to

be missing   & not missed but   in Ohio the stars sink   their fangs into the neck of the night   sky
& I am not afraid   of how you look   leaning into the dark   red   mercy is good lighting & a
hand   steady enough to hold the camera   still & I will take   whatever is coming & everything
after &
I   (laugh /   until / my head /   comes /

Off.)

HOW CAN BLACK PEOPLE WRITE ABOUT FLOWERS AT A TIME LIKE THIS

Forgive me, for I have been nurturing
my well-worn grudges against beauty.

I am hoping my neighbors will show some mercy
on me for backing my car
into the garden

& crushing what I will say were the peonies.
a flower with a short
season. born dying.

some might say it's a blessing to know your entrances
& exits. forgive me, for I have once again been recklessly

made responsible for the curation of softness
& have instead returned with another torrent

of viciousness. in the brief moment of their
flourish, at the opening of spring, I drove across
state lines

to gather peonies for a woman
who loved me once.
as a way of surrender,

I pull the already dying thing from the earth
in a mess of tangled knots & I insist
that you must keep it alive

for a year, even after it so desperately wants to be
done with the foolishness of its living.
The last thing I ask

of this relationship is to burden you with another
relationship. it is so delicious to define
the misery you are putting

a body out of. & just like that, we are talking about power.
how awful this must be for you I whispered as I closed my eyes
    & put the car into reverse.

THE GHOST OF MARVIN GAYE LEANS INTO A WALL OUTSIDE THE 7-ELEVEN AND TELLS YOU THE STORY OF HOW HE BROKE YOUR MAMA'S HEART REAL GOOD

I done showed up in enough dreams. I know how to make myself into anything. smokey said it ain't about the words. only about how you sing 'em. like you already got one foot in the grave. enough sex will make anyone give up on all that church shit. you thought I was good then. I'm somethin' else now. I can wear the moonlight as flesh. swear to god I'm bulletproof. lovers know I ain't good for a damn thing. but leaving a room loud and then empty. tell the women I still hear the ocean in my ears. in a body that holds nothing, I still cannot stop the water from filling my lungs. every time the sun sets.

IT IS AN ENTIRELY DIFFERENT THING TO WALK INTO THE RIVER WITH STONES

stretching the fabric of pockets stitched onto a black overcoat. It may seem like now is not the time
but shout out to the stones, whom the old lovers would drop a needle on the first morning they woke
to find out their beloved had run into the arms of another. Shout out to the snaps that firework &
flourish from a record's ridges in the silence before a song starts. An animal running its claws against
the bars of a prison long enough grows to love the sound more than it loves freedom. Mick Jagger
got a pregnant Merry Clayton out of bed at midnight because he needed someone to sing the word
murder like they were trying to squeeze it through a barbed wire fence without opening a wound on
their own fingers & Merry Clayton got home from the studio & miscarried & when her voice tears
at the air on the second syllable of *murder* Jagger whispers *wow* & the song must hold up despite
death & it must still be able to sell a car or a sandwich or a war no matter how many grains of sand it
kicked down the tunnel of the hourglass & it must be able to play in a market where two people trace
entire futures out of each other with a cascade of stolen glances. What backstory, what suffering are
you willing to make your soundtrack while pulling a zipper south or hiding a condom inside of a
hotel bible. Shout out never to my sins themselves, but always to the child they made me when I was
consumed by them. Shout out to the names of boys I wish were never born & how I've held each name
in my pocket & walked to the water's edge.

HOW CAN BLACK PEOPLE WRITE ABOUT FLOWERS AT A TIME LIKE THIS

i maybe should have mentioned before this cruel unfurling began:

i only believe in god so that i might have someone else to task

with the blistered fingers & the trench of guilt they are responsible for

placing in the direct center of any room where you desire

a shrinking of the distance between us. but it has been said

that the first carnation bloomed from a tear of the virgin

mary, which fell while jesus carried the cross with blood

streaming into his eyes. this is the part about a mother's

love. how i wore a carnation at the tip of a suit jacket on a night

a mother fought back tears & begged me not to do her daughter

wrong. & so here, let's make a deal. bring to me your palms

overflowing with the production of your most intemperate

anguish & i promise there is no target i will not stand in front of

for you. there is no wood that could fashion a cross to hold me.

LOVE YOUR NIGGAS

I am again considering how I sit inside of the space between two *gs*
as I did when the officer thumbed the handle of his weapon & asked

what you boys doing out so late one night on Livingston while the skin
of me & two of my niggas hushed the brightness of the streetlights

& we were old enough boys to know when someone wasn't actually
calling us *boys* & look at how these fools put dancing shoes on all that language

like my niggas ain't write the book & then have the book stolen & then
take back whatever pages they could before slipping out a window & what you have

to realize is that fire knows no master beyond whatever hands summoned it &
in virginia the torches sprayed a mist of sparks across the sky & in ohio me &

my niggas threw our hands over a fire & let the flame turn meat brown & cracked
jokes until somebody's mama got to rolling over in her grave & some niggas might say

to force movement out of the dead is another way to keep the ancestors close & so
I sin & I sin & I sin & I know & I hope when I die there are some niggas

still kicking it & willing to yell something heavy & improper about my living so that I too
may know what it is to roll over & to roll up on a nigga is another type of intimacy

& once, we rolled up on some niggas over a card game or over some weed or over

loneliness & I guess loneliness is another type of debt & there is no cure for the ache

of living like running with some niggas who might actually get your ass killed & speaking

of absence I am considering how the space between the two *gs* is where we might congregate

those who love us & those who want to see us dead. oh, how we've both found ourselves

wedded to the way the *g* sits in the back of the throat for a swift moment before tumbling

down the tongue & out of a car window in a town where you might be far away from your niggas &

I am wondering if this is the common ground I have been hearing so much about. It seems I love

my *gs* as you do, executioner. & what a tool this is for both of us. the way one can wrap their fingers

around the letter's open mouth & use its bottom to dig a grave. during the q&a, the old black

woman

who could be my kin in the way that anyone who has outlived my kin could be my kin asks me

what I think about putting the word *nigga* in my poems & in another voice, she is asking if I know

who had to die for me to be here with this ungrateful tongue & who am I to curate the small space

between love & violence & I think of this when I say *I love you nigga* & slap a hand so hard that the

blood vibrates underneath my palm for hours. I want the ghost of every type of love I have for my

niggas to echo for days like these, where it is raining in a city & I make mirrors out of every surface so that I am both me & all my niggas. & I am considering the *g* again. all my *g*s done dirt & some have become it. my *g*s wish to be made into ash upon their leaving but we bury my *g*s anyway. my niggas ain't ones to miss a chance to get fly & a funeral will do if nothing else will. god grant me a good grave in your gracious ground. let someone else be kept awake at night by the sound

of my body moving the earth in the name of my niggas & all of their breathing & iridescent sins.

A POEM IN WHICH I NAME THE BIRD

that circled above our heads in the leveled wheat field off route 39

where you wore white pants & upon the threshed wheat laid, as the border

between us, a quilt that once sprung from the fingers of your mother's mother

& that which will one day cover our bodies & to mask the sun,

there were two wings & I know the work of the poet is to say *bird*

or to say *wings* & not speak of their lineage but if I tell you that as a boy

on my grandmother's lap, we pointed to the sky at dusk & yelled the names of what cut

through the fat clouds on the way to somewhere south of the season we reckoned

with & if I tell you that once, the albatross stretched itself over the project rooftop

& the land was black but for the snow that fell for six whole months & there were no funerals

& everyone stayed inside with someone who kept them warm

& if I tell you all of this, lover I am reaching across the aching landscape to pull

close, then you must believe that in the wheat field, when we were together,

I knew well what could eclipse the burning

or I knew well what would give the blessing of shade,

a darkness over anything trying to take us from each other

HOW CAN BLACK PEOPLE WRITE ABOUT FLOWERS AT A TIME LIKE THIS

I knew not by the way I watched the cardinal kiss
the sticky neck of the ash tree from my window,

which had yet to become our window on a morning I
did not wake you due to how the time bends

forward around the parts of a country that keeps us
apart & I suppose I should have known by this but did not.

how, between us, I have always been the one able to see the future
& have still loved you in every version of it & I should have known

by you in the car & singing with the windows up & the highway's growl
sharp enough to drown out the lift of your voice. how you'd get a lyric wrong

& in my head, I rewrote the song to whatever you had newly determined
it to be & I did not know by how you rolled over right as the cardinal—covered

in the ruins of its labor—drifted away, the tree newly naked & stripped to
its barest layer. I only knew when thinking of Gram Parsons

& how a suit was sewn for him when he was 21 & on the suit there were bursts of red
poppy flowers & how the resin from the pod of the poppy makes morphine possible

& how Gram Parsons sat underneath a dark sky at Joshua Tree
when he was 26 & how he had been clean for months but wanted to see the stars

puff out their round cheeks over the sand that, in the darkness, must have looked like pearls
& I do not need to tell you that he did not survive the night, or the morphine

injected into him & to adorn yourself in the tools of your eventual undoing is not by itself
romance & to wear your demise across your own shoulders is not romance.

but, like the poppy, I have become something more dangerous than I was once
& this is how I have learned my heart's worst fears.

each small misery could be something that takes us away from each other.
I knew this way, too. I have dreams about planes crashing & houses on fire

& in the dream I am both the watcher & the sufferer. it can be said that this is love. to
imagine all of the worst separations. forgive me. I am being too literal again,

which all my most attractive friends say is not romantic. let me try something
else. love is not the drug itself but is the fluorescent palm that splits the earth

in the name of its blooming. not the drug, but the object so beautiful it demands
to be stitched into something that the body can consume.

or, here. what I meant to say when I could not bring myself to wake you.
I imagine the cardinal tears away the layers of that which holds it up to ensure everything

underneath is real. you leave and atop my sink a makeup remover holds a memory of
you & the toothbrush dripping the small pond into a contour of porcelain

holds a memory of you & the mug on the table with the stain of lipstick shaped
like the crescent of a blood moon holds a memory of you & I am sorry I couldn't do this

without talking about the dead & the songs they wrote. Gram Parsons had his body
set on fire at Joshua Tree & today people say the ashes still blow into their hair

& their eyes & god, what a miracle. all I have been trying to say is this:
may even the residue of our love find a curve of wind to dance an echo into.

THE GHOST OF MARVIN GAYE SITS INSIDE THE SHELL OF NIKOLA TESLA'S MACHINE AND BUILDS HIMSELF A PROPER COFFIN

shit where I'm from all you had
to do to make a man
                    disappear

          was give him the love of a good woman
          and a little temptation from a bad one

and that ain't a trick
of nothing except two

          stars snapping their fingers
          together at the right rhythm

and before you know it,
everybody gonna find themselves

          behind a new curtain.
          The first funeral is when you sweat

through a suit on stage and the women don't even bother
screaming. Everything that comes after is just waiting.

I seen the future too once and wasn't nothin' there

except a trail of broken hearts calling me *daddy*.

I seen progress and all I got is these empty rooms. Don't let
all that begging fool you, baby. I didn't never want forgiveness

or any type of heaven that didn't wash off with a sunrise.
I imagine in a field somewhere all the parts of myself I left behind

writhing themselves back together. And *that*'s the trick.
You make yourself a god to someone new

every night and then before you know it, you can write
your own bible. I was building a grave this whole time and you all

were too drunk on the howling of naked
skin to notice. It takes a man to go home
and die. It takes a man to drain the light from his mother's eyes
while blood makes the outline of a small boy's hand on her Sunday dress.

In this version of the gospel, the flood is already there.

In this version, Noah opens the doors to the ark and begs

the animals to come inside but they shake their

heads and march into the drowning one by one.

CUTTER: *Take a minute to consider your achievement. I once told you about a sailor who drowned.*

ROBERT ANGIER: *Yes, he said it was like going home.*

CUTTER: *I lied. He said it was agony.*

THE PRESTIGE

in the

                                    end

the

        only   arms

        offered

THE PRESTIGE

in the moments before the eruptions

of our cruelest corners pull us apart, friends,

remind me to tell you of the times I have seen

the way a good season has lingered in the

hopes of dancing along our faces one last

time, and how that has made me decide that

I must stay here, wretched as the staying

may feel. only the fool arms themself

with the tools of undoing and nothing

beyond. I want to die a little less than I did

yesterday and a little less than I did the day

before. offered the chance to make amends

will open

to the hollow

and un   known

darkness

for what we have endured together,

I will open the hidden vault: all heartbreak

is a descendant of the untouched

imagination. into the hollow void I've left

I echo the names of all who have pulled me

from the depths of my own design.

and underneath the known haunting

of invented darkness, I promise you

it isn't all that bad. we can all mourn

until the mourning trembles out a celebration.

ACKNOWLEDGEMENTS

Thanks to the following journals for publishing previous versions of these poems:

"HOW CAN BLACK PEOPLE WRITE ABOUT FLOWERS AT A TIME LIKE THIS" in *Poem-a-Day*, *Academy of American Poets*

"WATCHING A FIGHT AT THE NEW HAVEN DOG PARK, FIRST TWO DOGS AND THEN THEIR OWNERS" and "IF LIFE IS AS SHORT AS OUR ANCESTORS INSIST IT IS, WHY ISN'T EVERYTHING I WANT ALREADY AT MY FEET" in *Narrative Northeast*

"WELCOME TO HEARTBREAK" and "THE GHOST OF MARVIN GAYE SITS IN THE RUINS OF THE OLD LIVINGSTON FLEA MARKET AND CONSIDERS MONOGAMY" in *Frontier Poetry*

"I TEND TO THINK FORGIVENESS LOOKS THE WAY IT DOES IN THE MOVIES" and "NONE OF MY VICES ARE VIOLENT ENOUGH TO UNDO REMEMBERING" in *wildness*

"IT'S NOT LIKE NIKOLA TESLA KNEW ALL OF THOSE PEOPLE WERE GOING TO DIE" and "FOR THE DOGS WHO BARKED AT ME ON THE SIDEWALKS IN CONNECTICUT" in *PoetryNow* and *Poetry*

"YOU ABOUT TO TELL HER YOU LOVE HER, WE OFF THAT" and "IT'S NOT LIKE NIKOLA TESLA KNEW ALL OF THOSE PEOPLE WERE GOING TO DIE" in *Denver Quarterly*

"HOW CAN BLACK PEOPLE WRITE ABOUT FLOWERS AT A TIME LIKE THIS" in *Sixth Finch*

"IT IS MAYBE TIME TO ADMIT THAT MICHAEL JORDAN DEFINITELY PUSHED OFF" in *Southern Indiana Review*

"GLAMOUR ON THE WEST STREETS / SILVER OVER EVERYTHING" in *ReCap*

"THE GHOST OF MARVIN GAYE STANDS OVER HIS FATHER'S GRAVE AND FORGETS TO ASK FOR AN APOLOGY" and "MAN IT'S SO HARD NOT TO ACT RECKLESS" in *The Arkansas International*

"HOW CAN BLACK PEOPLE WRITE ABOUT FLOWERS AT A TIME LIKE THIS" and "HOW CAN BLACK PEOPLE WRITE ABOUT FLOWERS AT A TIME LIKE THIS" in *Boulevard*

"IT OCCURS TO ME THAT I AM LOVED MOST FOR THE THINGS I REFUSE," "A POEM IN WHICH I NAME THE BIRD" and "HOW CAN BLACK PEOPLE WRITE ABOUT FLOWERS AT A TIME LIKE THIS" in *The Collagist*

Waves and waves of gratitude to everyone at Tin House who believed in this project, and fought for it to have the best life it could possibly have. Sorry I was so bad at fantasy basketball.

I owe an impossible debt to the artists and activists in Columbus, Ohio who welcomed me back and allowed me to once again fold into a community I'd known and loved for so long. My dearest friends Meaghan, Stephanie, Sam, Madison, Mia, and everyone else who spent time with me in my first two years back home. Dominique Larue, Carried By 6, Cameron Granger, Hakim Callwood, Marshall Shorts, Kim Leddy, Mosaic, The Coalition To Free Masonique Saunders, Sharon Udoh, Phil Kim, Kate Sweeney, BQIC, Julia Oller, Vada Azeem, Jeni Britton Bauer. The poetry and writing community in Columbus—who I am lucky enough to also call friends: William Evans, Izetta Thomas, Eric and Eliza Obenauf, Brett Gregory, Tom Konitzer, Ruth Awad, Elissa Washuta, Steve Abbott, Rose Smith, Scott Woods, Rachel Wiley, Barbara Fant, Nick White, Hannah Stephenson, Maggie Smith, Paige Webb, Dionne Custer Edwards.

To my many communities beyond this city I love, and the people who have offered friendship and guidance when they surely didn't have to: Eve Ewing, who has never not had my back. Angel, Kaveh, Fatimah, and Safia. How lucky to have you all as siblings. Danez, Jeremy, Jayson, Nabila, Desiree, Jerriod, Liz, Paula, Jacqui, Hieu, Anis, Carly, Keegan, Ron Villanueva, Morgan Parker, Saeed Jones, Tommy Pico, Molly Bess Rector, Omar Holmon, Molly Rose Quinn, sam sax, Phillip B. Williams, Ocean Vuong, Jonny Sun, Mark Cugini, Layne Ransom, Raymond Antrobus, Peter Kahn, Franny Choi, Crystal Salas, David Hall, Tory Weber, Andy Grace, and all of the Kenyon Young Writers, Kieran Collier, Vann Newkirk, Josie Duffy, Diamond Sharp, Gabrielle Bates, Luther Hughes, Isaac Fitzgerald, Raena Shirali, Cameron Awkward-Rich, Camonghne Felix, Julian Randall, Frank Johnson, Erica Dawson, Paige Lewis, Melissa Febos, Tyree Daye, Emily Jungmin Yoon, Kendra DeColo, Dan Campbell, Jess Rizkallah, Julien Baker, Tiana Clark, Jessica Hopper, Lucy Dacus, Adam Falkner, Monica Sok, Shira Erlichman, Ashley Ford, Alison Rollins, Dujie Tahat, Tochi Onyebuchi, Shea Serrano, Lilliam Rivera, Mary Choi, Ian Blair, Angela Flournoy, Jason Parham, Juan Vidal, Donika Kelly, and countless others who have played a role in carrying me the past three years.

To the Lyrics N' Layups Basketball Group Chat: Ben & Scott & Nate & Cortney & José & Erika & Hannah & Zain & Pedro & Kaveh (again.) Thanks for letting me spend most of my procrastinating moments rambling about sports.

There are many writers who have been lighthouses for me, whether they know it or not: Ross Gay, Terrance Hayes, Rita Dove, Natasha Trethewey, Carolyn Forché, Sharon Olds, Ilya Kaminsky, Adrian Matejka, Greil Marcus, Khadijah Queen, francine j. harris, and Tracy K. Smith.

To Tabia, Royal, and the team at BEOTIS for keeping my head on straight.

To the memories of Amber Evans, MarShawn McCarrel, Bill Hurley, Gina Blaurock, and Rubén Castilla Herrera.

And to Eloisa, who I remain lucky enough to uncover new curiosities with.

PHOTO © KATE SWEENEY

HANIF ABDURRAQIB is a poet, essayist, and cultural critic from Columbus, Ohio. His poetry has been published in *PEN American*, *Muzzle*, *Vinyl*, and other journals, and his essays and criticism have been published in *The New Yorker*, *Pitchfork*, *The New York Times*, and *Fader*. His first full-length poetry collection, *The Crown Ain't Worth Much*, was named a finalist for the Eric Hoffer Book Award and nominated for a Hurston/Wright Legacy Award. His first collection of essays, *They Can't Kill Us Until They Kill Us*, was named a book of the year by NPR; *Esquire*; BuzzFeed; *O, The Oprah Magazine*; *Pitchfork*; and *Chicago Tribune*, among others. *Go Ahead in the Rain: Notes to a Tribe Called Quest* was a *New York Times* bestseller, a National Book Critics Circle Award finalist, a Kirkus Prize finalist, and was longlisted for the National Book Award. In 2021, he was named a MacArthur "Genius Grant" Fellow and published *A Little Devil in America: In Praise of Black Performance*, a finalist for the National Book Award, which was awarded the Andrew Carnegie Medal for Excellence in Nonfiction. He is a graduate of Beechcroft High School.